I0797538

PAUL POGBA

BY MICHAEL DECKER

WORLD'S GREATEST SOCCER PLAYERS

SportsZone

An Imprint of Abdo Publishing
abdobooks.com

abdobooks.com

Published by Abdo Publishing, a division of ABDO, PO Box 398166, Minneapolis, Minnesota 55439.

Printed in the United States of America, North Mankato, Minnesota
092019
012020

Cover Photo: Martin Meissner/AP Images
Interior Photos: Kyodo/AP Images, 4; Martin Meissner/AP Images, 7, 22; David Klein/Sportimage/Cal Sports Media/AP Images, 9; Catarina Belova/Shutterstock Images, 10; Rich von Biberstein/Icon Sportswire/AP Images, 13; Matthew Peters/Manchester United/Getty Images, 14; Massimo Pinca/AP Images, 16; Laurentvu/Taamallah/Sipa/AP Images, 19; Andres Kudacki/AP Images, 20; Simon Bellis/Cal Sports Media/AP Images, 25; Lahalle/Sipa/AP Images, 26; Ash Donelon/Manchester United/Getty Images, 29

Editor: Patrick Donnelly
Series Designer: Craig Hinton

Library of Congress Control Number: 2019942111

Publisher's Cataloging-in-Publication Data

Names: Decker, Michael, author.
Title: Paul Pogba / by Michael Decker
Description: Minneapolis, Minnesota : Abdo Publishing, 2020 | Series: World's greatest soccer players | Includes online resources and index.
Identifiers: ISBN 9781532190667 (lib. bdg.) | ISBN 9781644943458 (pbk.) | ISBN 9781532176517 (ebook)
Subjects: LCSH: Pogba, Paul, 1993- --Juvenile literature. | FC United of Manchester (Soccer team)--Juvenile literature. | European football--Biography--Juvenile literature. | Soccer players--Biography--Juvenile literature. | Professional athletes--Biography--Juvenile literature.
Classification: DDC 796.3340922--dc23

TABLE OF CONTENTS

CHAPTER
ONE

COMING THROUGH

Paul Pogba, star midfielder for the French men's national team, gained possession at his own end of the field. As defenders sprinted toward him, he launched the ball toward the opponents' goal. The ball skipped past a defender. Pogba's teammate Kylian Mbappe caught up to it and dribbled toward the net, with Pogba trailing him. Little did Pogba know that he'd just set himself up for one of the biggest moments of his career.

Pogba and France were leading Croatia 2–1 in the second half of the 2018 World Cup final. France reached

Paul Pogba stepped up for France in a huge moment during the 2018 World Cup final.

the final with Pogba playing a key supporting role in the central midfield. Now he had a chance to help his team on the offensive end with more than just his passing skills.

IMPORTANT FIRST GOAL

Pogba played a huge role in France's first victory of the 2018 World Cup. In the 80th minute of the match against Australia, Pogba approached the net and poked a loose ball high into the air. The ball sailed over the goalkeeper, deflected off the bottom of the crossbar, and landed just over the goal line. The ball had glanced off an Australia defender, making it officially an own goal. But it gave France a 2–1 victory.

Pogba got into position near the top of the box. Mbappe passed to teammate Antoine Griezmann, who redirected the ball back to Pogba. The towering French midfielder fired a right-footed shot.

The ball bounced off a Croatia defender. But it rolled back near Pogba. He quickly gathered it and shot again, this time with his left foot. The ball rocketed past the defense and the goalkeeper, who got caught leaning the wrong way. Pogba's goal put France ahead 3–1.

Pogba is mobbed by his teammates after he extended France's lead to 3–1.

It ended up being the game-winner as France won 4–2 and captured the 2018 World Cup.

Pogba entered the 2018 World Cup as one of the most popular soccer players in the world. But during most of the tournament, he wasn't the star scoring all the goals. He played an important role helping as a midfielder. He helped France get the ball out of its own end and made passes that set up the offense. When Pogba got an opportunity to score in the final, he didn't waste it. These skills are what make Pogba one of the world's best soccer players.

Pogba celebrates after his first World Cup title.

FFF

CHAPTER TWO

MAKING A NAME FOR HIMSELF

Paul Pogba was born in Lagny-sur-Marne, a suburb of Paris, on March 15, 1993. His parents had left the West African country of Guinea to look for more work opportunities in France. Paul's parents divorced when he was two years old. He lived with his mother after the divorce but remained close with his father, who lived nearby.

Paul played soccer near his home with his twin brothers, Mathias and Florentin. They are two years older than Paul. The brothers spent hours playing together and with other friends. Most of the kids were older than Paul.

Paul was born and raised in a suburb of Paris.

Playing with them helped Paul quickly improve, and soon he was better than many of the older kids.

ALL IN THE FAMILY

Paul's brothers have also played soccer professionally. Florentin has played in pro leagues in France and Turkey as well as with Atlanta United of Major League Soccer (MLS). Mathias has also played professionally in France. Unlike Paul, Florentin and Mathias play internationally for Guinea instead of France.

Paul began playing organized soccer at age six. He joined US Roissy-en-Brie, his local club team. Paul continued to play with older kids. He also spent a lot of time practicing his skills. He once spent two days teaching himself to juggle the ball 50 times with each foot and 50 times with his head. He also was very competitive and did whatever he could to help his team win.

The coaches at Roissy believed Paul needed to go to a bigger team to reach his full potential. Paul joined US Torcy, the best youth soccer club in his area. After one

Paul's brother Florentin makes a play for Atlanta United in 2019.

season there, Le Havre—a professional team based a few hours away—lured Paul away to join their team. Le Havre had a reputation for developing good young players.

AIG
MANCHESTER UNITED

Paul soon added his name to that list. In fact, he soon stood out so much that Manchester United called. The English club was one of the biggest in the world. Now it wanted Paul to join its youth system. Though he was only 16 years old, Paul decided it was an opportunity he could not turn down.

Paul made the jump to England to play for Manchester United when he was just 16 years old.

SERIE A
TIM
6

CHAPTER
THREE

TO ITALY AND BACK

After two seasons playing in Manchester United's youth system, Pogba got called up to the senior team during the 2011–12 season. He struggled to break into the lineup, however, and spent most of the time on the bench. Unhappy with the situation at Manchester United, Pogba left to join Juventus, one of the most successful clubs in Italy.

Pogba found the opportunity he was looking for at Juventus. Though he was just 19 years old, he quickly established himself as a key central midfielder on the

Pogba quickly became an impact player for Juventus.

veteran-laden team. Often lining up next to superstar Andrea Pirlo, Pogba helped lead Juventus to league championships in 2013 and 2014. In between, he helped France win the 2013 Under-20 World Cup.

At just 21 years old, Pogba was one of the brightest young stars in Europe. His status grew in the summer of 2014. Pogba starred for France at the World Cup in Brazil. Against Nigeria in the Round of 16, Pogba broke a scoreless tie late in the game as he headed a ball into the net. France won the match 2–0. France bowed out in the quarterfinals, but Pogba was recognized as the tournament's Best Young Player.

Few players in the world could match Pogba's combination of athleticism and technical skills. His dribbling and passing abilities helped Juventus control the ball. On defense, Pogba excelled at shutting down the

Pogba came on strong for France in the 2014 World Cup.

Jeep
6
Jeep
15

opposition's best players. He had a rocket of a shot, too. And he was able to make plays all across the field.

That showed again in the spring of 2015. Playing on the road at Real Madrid, Pogba set up a goal that sent Juventus to the Champions League final. Although the team lost to Barcelona in that match, which determined the top team in Europe, Pogba's stock continued to grow. Two more league titles in 2015 and 2016 helped, too. However, Pogba was ready for a new challenge. There was no shortage of teams looking to provide one.

POPULAR OFF THE FIELD

Aside from being a great soccer player, Pogba also gained fans from his social media accounts. In 2019 he had more than 35 million followers on Instagram. He often posts about soccer and fashion, which is something he's also passionate about. Pogba also changes his hairstyle regularly.

Pogba and his Juventus teammates celebrate after beating Real Madrid in the 2015 Champions League semifinals.

CHAPTER **FOUR**

UPS AND DOWNS

With many of the world's biggest clubs seeking to sign Pogba, he had one more opportunity to make a big statement in the summer of 2016. France was hosting that year's European Championships, and with Pogba leading a talented French team, many expected them to win.

However, Pogba struggled early on. He was also criticized for his lack of discipline. As the tournament continued, Pogba began playing better. He scored a key goal on a header in the quarterfinals. Then he helped lead the team past Germany, the defending World Cup

Pogba and France came up just short against Portugal in the 2016 European Championships.

champions, in the semifinal. But the tournament ended in more disappointment, as Portugal upset France in the final.

The uneven performance didn't turn teams off Pogba, though. After all, he was still only 23 years old. That August, Manchester United paid €105 million ($116 million) to bring the midfielder back to England. That was a record transfer fee at the time.

After his first experience in Manchester, Pogba was eager to show that he could thrive in England. And at times he did. In 2017 he helped Manchester United win the Europa League. That is a second-tier competition among European teams. However, after their club paid so much for Pogba, United fans had high expectations. And in 2017–18, Pogba struggled to live up to them. Manchester United manager Jose Mourinho accused Pogba of not

Pogba returned to Manchester United in 2016.

adidas
CHEVROLET

Pogba and Kante helped France dominate the middle of the field at the World Cup.

showing enough discipline, especially on defense. So he subbed Pogba out in situations where a star would normally play a bigger role.

Going into the 2018 World Cup, many wondered if Pogba could still be the star on a championship team. Many also wondered how he would accept his role. On the talented French team, Pogba was asked to play a disciplined role as a defensive midfielder. Some doubted he could do it. But playing alongside N'Golo Kante, Pogba and France had one of the tournament's stingiest defenses. And with his goal in the final, Pogba showed he was still one of the world's best all-around players.

FACING CRITICISM

Throughout his career, Pogba has dealt with criticism no matter where he played. The criticism increased when he struggled with Manchester United. Writers and analysts said Pogba got too much money when he signed with the club. Pogba described himself as the most criticized player in the world during the World Cup. He also said he tries to not read the criticism from writers or fans.

Back in Manchester, Mourinho was fired midway through the 2018–19 season. Pogba had more freedom to attack under the system installed by new manager Ole Gunnar Solskjær.

And he responded with a career-high 13 goals in Premier League matches.

But once again he yearned for a change of scenery. That summer he was rumored to be headed to any number of the world's biggest teams. Real Madrid reportedly expressed interest. Juventus appeared to be open to a reunion with their former midfield star.

However, in the end, Manchester United decided to hold onto one of its most valuable assets. When the European transfer window closed on September 2, Pogba was still in Manchester. He would be a big part of United's push to return to the top of the Premier League.

Though transfer rumors swirled around Pogba all summer, he was back with Manchester United for the start of the 2019–20 season.

adidas
adidas

GLOSSARY

club

The team a player competes with outside of his or her national team.

midfielder

A player who stays mostly in the middle third of the field and links the defenders with the forwards.

own goal

A goal that is last touched by a defender before it crosses the goal line.

semifinal

The second-to-last round of play in a tournament; the winner of a semifinal game advances to the championship.

transfer fee

The amount of money paid by one club to another for the right to sign one of its players to a contract.

transfer window

A period of time in which players can change teams.

veteran

A player who has played many years.

World Cup

The biggest soccer tournament in the world, held once every four years among national teams.

MORE INFORMATION

BOOKS

Karpovich, Todd. *Manchester United*. Minneapolis, MN: Abdo Publishing, 2018.

Marthaler, Jon. *Ultimate Soccer Road Trip*. Minneapolis, MN: Abdo Publishing, 2019.

Moussavi, Sam. *World Cup Heroes*. Minneapolis, MN: Abdo Publishing, 2019.

ONLINE RESOURCES

To learn more about Paul Pogba, please visit **abdobooklinks.com** or scan this QR code. These links are routinely monitored and updated to provide the most current information available.

INDEX

ABOUT THE AUTHOR

Originally from a small town in the Upper Peninsula of Michigan, Michael Decker has spent his career as a children's book author writing about various sports such as soccer. He lives in Laramie, Wyoming, with his wife, three kids, and his dog, Emily.